ISBN 1-902571-06-1

Gilbert Deya Publishing
24 Manor Grove
London SE15 1SX
Tel: (+44) 207 358 0303
Fax: (+44) 207 639 9603
Email: gilbertdeya@yahoo.com

Dangerous Prayers To Break Satan's Forces

by

ARCHBISHOP GILBERT DEYA

INTRODUCTION

The prayers in this book are for battling with evil spirits and cause people to live under the bondage of satan. Prayers are to be used daily for individual needs, for example, to pray against bad luck, sigleness, separation, divorce, financially difficulties and spiritual problems. These dangerous prayers destroy satan's forces instantly,awake the ignorant and teach how to approach God . When you are praying please make sure you repeant, refresh and you have to be aware that your fighting spritual forces of darkness. You will definately through overcome all the problems facing you at all times in Jesus name. Amen!The Charismatic Christians are those who speak in tongues while praying in mass, they are also known as Pentecostals. Pentecost came to being from the day the Holy Spirit came upon believers on the day of the of the Pentecost, when all the people who were in Solomon's porch had a mass prayer and speaking in tongues.Nowadays even though they pray in mass and in tongues, their prayers are not effective because they don't apply wisdomand knowledge, using the blood of Jesus while they are praying.

Prayers move mountains which are problems, problems are discribed as mountains, if you are having problems, those problems are mountains into your life. The question is what is your mountain? Face your problems with dangerous prayer and overcome them . As you pray, the Holy Spirit will reveal his power and give you the knowledge of prayer. Do not let satan destroy your house, family and community.Use this book of dangerous prayers daily. When facing problems go straight to the prayer relevant to your problem and use it to communicate with God in an accepted manner so that God's will be done in your life. Dangerous are effective to all evil forces assigned to destroy people's lives.

CONTENTS

Prayers to destroy the powers that cause sexual immorality and family destruction

Personal prayers to specific problems in your life

Confession

Archbishop Gilbert Deya

**Personal prayers for attacking the devil
and putting the whole armour of God**

FIRST PRAYER

Twenty-one prayers for sending back evil to the sender in Jesus' name

1. I destroy evil spirits sent by my enemies to destroy my entire family, by the blood of Jesus. Let their powers be consumed by the Holy Spirit forever. Amen.

2. I destroy all the evil powers that have caused confusion in my family. I destroy you by the blood of Jesus. May those evil spirits go back to the sender in Jesus' name.

3. I destroy all the powers of darkness used by witches to confuse my life, by the blood of Jesus. And let those witches die before they kill me. They must die, die, die and never attack anybody.

4. I destroy the works of all evil powers sent by the witches and wizards in the day or at night, by the blood of Jesus and I command them to go back to kill those who have sent them.

5. I destroy all satanic forces sent by my neighbours, to terminate my life, by the blood of Jesus and may these forces destroy those who sent them.

6. I destroy every evil spirit, which has been sent or will be sent by wicked people to confuse my family, by the blood of Jesus I command them to go back to those who sent them. Amen.

7. I destroy the works and plans of the satanic forces sent by my relatives to separate me from my family, by the blood of Jesus. May my relatives be united in love in Jesus' name.

8. I destroy all the evil powers attacking me in the night or in the day, sent by my enemies to kill me, by the blood of Jesus. Let all their weapons be destroyed in Jesus' name.

9. I destroy all demonic powers used by people around me to kill me, by the blood of Jesus. I command them to go back to the sender, back to the sender, back to the sender in Jesus' name.

10. I destroy the works and plans of all evil spirits, powers of darkness, and satanic forces organised against me and sent by evil people. I destroy them, by the blood of Jesus. Let them not see me but go back to the senders.

11. I destroy the spirits of the devil sent by satanic forces to sleep with me at night. Let them die! die! die! and not come back again to sleep with me. Amen.

12. I destroy the wicked people's spells and jinxes from the powers of darkness wishing me dead. I destroy them, by the blood of Jesus. Let their wickedness perish! perish! perish! in Jesus' name.

13. I destroy every weapon of the devil planned against me, by witches and wizards, by the blood of Jesus. May those weapons of the devil go back to sender and destroy the senders, in Jesus' name.

14. I destroy all kinds of sickness Satan sent to me, by the blood of Jesus. May the power of sickness be nullified before reaching me.

15. I destroy the spirit of cancer planned to affect my family, by the blood of Jesus. Spirit of cancer you must die! die! die! and not touch any member of my family again.

16. I destroy all plans and intentions of the devil to affect my family, by the blood of Jesus and let them be confused and perish for ever, in Jesus' name.

17. I destroy all the diseases affecting people that may be planned to reach my family, by the blood of Jesus. May the diseases disappear on their way and die forever.

18. I destroy powers of darkness that affect my finances, by the blood of Jesus. May the Lord have mercy on me and abundantly prosper my family in Jesus' name.

19. I destroy all spirits of lack that have been directed to affect my finances, by the blood of Jesus. The spirit of lack must not find me. May the glory of the Lord cover me in Jesus name.

20. I destroy all secret plans of the wicked people against me, by the blood of Jesus. May all the plans raised against me go back to the sender and destroy those who had sent them.

21. I destroy all secret things and plans of the evil people against me, by the blood of Jesus. May the evil people perish with their evil plans before they affect me in Jesus name.

**Personal prayers for attacking the devil and
putting on the whole armour of God**

SECOND PRAYER.

*Sending evil spirits back
to the sender*

This prayer, from Psalm 35, is for spiritual
warfare. When using this prayer, know that
what you utter is affecting the evil kingdom
and whatsoever is planned against you, is
sent back to the sender.

Psalms 35: 1-28.
*Oppose those who oppose me, Lord, and
fight those who fight against me!*

*Take your shield and armour and come to
my rescue.*

Lift up your spear and war axe against those who pursue me. Promise that you will save me.

May those who try to kill me be defeated and disgraced! May those who plot against me be turned back and confused!

May they be like straw blown by the wind as the angel of the Lord pursues them!

May their path be dark and slippery while the angel of the Lord strikes them down!

Without any reason they laid a trap for me and dug a deep hole to catch me.

But destruction will catch them before they know it; they will be caught in their own trap and fall to their destruction!

Then I will be glad because of the Lord; I will be happy because he saved me.

With all my heart I will say to the Lord, "There is no one like you. You protect the weak from the strong, the poor from the oppressor."

Evil people testify against me and accuse me of crimes I know nothing about.

They pay me back evil for good, and I sink in despair.

But when they were sick, I dressed in mourning; I deprived myself of food;

I prayed with my head bowed low, as I would pray for a friend or a brother. I went around bent over in mourning, as one who mourns for his mother.

But when I was in trouble, they were all glad and gathered around to make fun of me; strangers beat me and kept striking me.

Like those who would mock a cripple, they glared at me with hate.

How much longer, Lord, will you just look on? Rescue me from their attacks; save my life from these lions!

Then I will thank you in the assembly of your people; I will praise you before them all.

Don't let my enemies, those liars, gloat over my defeat. Don't let those who hate me for no reason smirk with delight over my sorrow.

They do not speak in a friendly way; instead they invent all kinds of lies about peace-loving people.

They accuse me, shouting, "We saw what you did!"

But you, O Lord, have seen this. So don't be silent, Lord; don't keep yourself far away!

Rouse yourself, O Lord, and defend me; rise up, my God, and plead my cause.

You are righteous, O Lord, so declare me innocent; don't let my enemies gloat over me.

Don't let them say to themselves, "We are rid of him! That's just what we wanted!"

May those who gloat over my suffering be completely defeated and confused; may those who claim to be better than I am be covered with shame and disgrace.

May those who want to see me acquitted shout for joy and say again and again,

"How great is the Lord! He is pleased with the success of his servant."

Then I will proclaim your righteousness, and I will praise you all day long.'

Prayers for attacking the devil and putting on the whole armour of God

THIRD PRAYER.

Destroying thousands of enemies around you

This prayer is taken from Psalms 3, and it is useful as a start to daily prayers. These dangerous prayers will reverse your situation against your enemies.

Psalms 3.
"I have so many enemies, Lord, so many who turn against me! They talk about me and say, "God will not help him." But you, O Lord, are always my shield from danger; you give me victory and restore my courage. I call to the Lord for help, and from his sacred hill, he answers me."

"I lie down and sleep, and all night long the Lord <u>protects me</u>. I am not afraid of the thousands of enemies who surround me on every side. Come, Lord! Save me, my God! You punish all my enemies and leave them powerless to harm me. Victory comes from the Lord- may he bless his people." Amen

Personal prayer for attacking the devil and putting on the whole armour of God

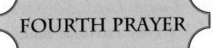

FOURTH PRAYER

Prayers when the spirit of death is surrounding you

(or anyone in your family who is facing death)

Father, I come to you in the name of Jesus Christ. Death has taken most of my family members. Few of us are left. Everybody is passing away. Maybe they died because our grandparents sinned and we have offended you. I repent the sins of my grandparents, my mother, my father and the sins that make Satan to destroy , kill and finish us.

In the name of Jesus Christ, Lord, forgive me and save my soul. Deliver me from death. Deliver me from famine. Deliver me from the problems that are facing the nations of the world. Now take care of me, and control me.

King of Kings, Son of the living God, your blood is powerful. Now I apply your blood to my life and to the life of my family. Protect me and keep me alive. Let me see many more days to come. And I know the spirit of lack shall never be upon me. I fear nothing because I know that Jesus covers me. Now, death, stop! I rebuke you and bind your powers, in Jesus' name.

You will never touch me.
You will never touch me.
You will never kill me.
You will never destroy me.
Because the blood of Jesus, is upon me.
I speak to death, 'death you are finished!
Your powers are destroyed!
You will never touch me!
I will fear you no more!
I take the seal of the Holy Spirit by faith.

The anointing of the Holy Spirit will cover me all the days of my life and no premature death shall be upon my life in Jesus' name. Amen.
I will fear no evil, nor will I fear death. From today onwards, I am the redeemed of the Lord in Jesus' name. Amen.

Personal prayers for attacking the devil and putting on the whole armour of God

FIFTH PRAYER

Prayer to destroy the spirit of death in Jesus"name

This prayer is taken from the Book of **Psalms 18** and it is used to release fire of the Holy Spirit to destroy the spirit of death.

Psalm 18: 1-30.
I love you, O LORD, my strength. The LORD is my rock, my fortress and my deliverer; my God is my rock, in whom, I take refuge.

He is my shield and the horn of my salvation, my stronghold. I call to the LORD, who is worthy of praise, and I am saved from my enemies. The cords of death entangled me; the torrents of destruction overwhelmed me. The cords of the grave, coiled around me; the snares of death confronted me. In my distress I called to the LORD; I cried to my God for help.

From his temple he heard my voice, my cry came before him, into his ears. The earth trembled and quaked, and the foundations of the mountains shook; they trembled because he was angry. Smoke rose from his nostrils; consuming fire came from his mouth, burning coals blazed out of it. He parted the heavens and came down; dark clouds were under his feet. He mounted the cherubim and flew; he soared on the wings of the wind.

He made darkness his covering, his canopy around him- the dark rain clouds of the sky. Out of the brightness of his presence clouds advanced, with hailstones and bolts of lightning. The LORD thundered from heaven; the voice of the Most High resounded.

He shot his arrows and scattered the enemies, great bolts of lightning and routed them. The valleys of the sea were exposed and the foundations of the earth laid bare at your rebuke, O LORD, at the blast of breath from your nostrils.

He reached down from on high and took hold of me; he drew me out of deep waters. They confronted me in the day of my disaster, but the LORD was my support. He brought me out into a spacious place; he rescued me because he delighted in me.

The LORD has dealt with me according to my righteousness; according to the cleanness of my hands he has rewarded me. For I have kept the ways of the LORD; I have not done evil by turning from my God.

All his laws are before me; I have not turned away from his decrees. I have been blameless before him and have kept myself from sin. The LORD has rewarded me according to my righteousness, according to the cleanness of my hands in his sight. To the faithful you show yourself faithful, to the blameless you show yourself blameless, to the pure you show yourself pure, but to the crooked you show yourself shrewd. You save the humble but bring low those whose eyes are haughty.

You, O LORD, keep my lamp burning; my God turns my darkness into light.

With your help I can advance against a troop, with my God I can scale a wall. As for God, his way is perfect; the word of the LORD is flawless.

He is a shield for all who take refuge in him.

Personal prayers for attacking the devil and putting the whole armour of God

SIXTH PRAYER

Prayers when you are around wicked people

May the Lord give me protection forever and fight against evil people around me.

May all the wicked people who meet and plan evil against me get confused and their evil plans turn against them.

May the Lord's love surround me and my family with his glorious power and destroy every wicked spirit around them.

May all the witches and wizards who plan death against me die now before their plans reach me.

May death not see any of my family but return to the sender.

The Lord is my shepherd, whom shall I fear? I am standing on the Rock; on the anointing of the Holy Spirit, on the power of my Saviour.

These wicked people that surround me day and night, who try to destroy my life and to kill me, I am above your destruction because I am born again, and the Holy Ghost is in me.

I am dangerous as Moses was to the Egyptians in Egypt.

The magicians performed their petty miracles, but Moses' miracles were greater and so powerful that they swallowed up the miracles of the magicians of Egypt.

That is how the anointing on my life must swallow the witches' power, in Jesus' name.

They shall not destroy me, but their evil shall go back to them and destroy them.

Glory be to Jesus, the Son of the living God who has given me power to become a child of God.

I am a child of God through Jesus Christ. No weapon can be raised against me because I am a child of God.

I am dangerous to the wicked people that surround me. Thank you God, I am born again.

Thank you God for Jesus.

Through His tender mercies, I am a true child of God.

Hallelujah, Hallelujah! I am born again. And I have the anointing of the Holy Spirit in me. I am more than a conqueror.

I have conquered the wicked people who planned to kill me.

They will never, never, prevail. Victory is mine in Jesus' name.

Let all the wicked people be confused and their wickedness kill them.

Let all the wicked spirits among those who attack me perish.

Let whosoever wants to kill me die before his or her mission reaches me. Amen.

Personal prayers for attacking the devil and putting on the whole armour of God

SEVENTH PRAYER

Nine Prayers Against Secret Plans of the Devil

1   I destroy all the plans of the wicked people against my family's finances, by the blood of Jesus. May all wicked people die and the prosperity of the Lord prevail in me.

2   I destroy all the secret plans of my enemies against my married life, by the blood of Jesus. May the Lord bless my marriage but let the wickedness of the enemy be consumed by the Holy Spirit.

3   I destroy all the secret plans against all my children, by the blood of Jesus. May

the Lord lift my children higher than my enemies, in Jesus' name.

4   I destroy all the secret plans against me that make me not to prosper, by the blood of Jesus. May the Lord bless me everywhere I go and my enemies disappear by their own wickedness.

5   I destroy all the secret plans against me by my workmates, by the blood of Jesus. May the Lord bless me at work and all my enemies perish. May the fire of the Holy Ghost consume my enemies. May the Lord send fear to them and let them run away from me and die. Let their wicked power, die, die. Amen.

6   I destroy all secret plans against all what I am doing, by the blood of Jesus. May the Lord bless the work of my hands and prosper me above all my enemies.

7   I destroy all the secret plans of the people around me against my success, by the blood of Jesus. May the Holy Spirit protect me and lead my life to success, let me be the head but not the tail. Let me be richer than my enemies.

8.   I destroy all the secret plans of witches and wizards sent to confuse me, by the blood of Jesus. Let their wicked plans of confusion go back to them and confuse them in all their plans. Let their power perish. Let their power die. Let their power be destroyed and be consumed by the Holy Spirit.

9   I destroy all the secret plans to confuse my brain, by the blood of Jesus. May the Lord control my brain and give me wisdom and knowledge above my enemies.

Personal prayers for attacking the devil and putting on the whole armour

EIGHTH PRAYER

Releasing punishment to those who want to kill you

This prayer is taken from **Psalms 28**. It is aimed to send punishment to those who are your enemies and those who want to kill you. What you say in these Psalms will happen to the evil people, do not doubt it. You must know that the Lord is protecting you by fighting against your enemies

Psalms 28: 1-9;
"To you I call, O LORD my Rock; do not turn a deaf ear to me."

For if you remain silent,   I will be like those who have gone down to the pit.

Hear my cry for mercy as I call to you for help, as I lift up my hands toward your

Most Holy Place. Do not drag me away with the wicked, with those who do evil, who speak cordially with their neighbours but harbour malice in their hearts.

Repay them for their deeds and for their evil work; repay them for what their hands have done and bring back upon them what they deserve.

Since they show no regard for the works of the LORD and what his hands have done, he will tear them down and never build them up again.

Praise be to the LORD, for he has heard my cry for mercy.

The LORD is my strength and my shield; my heart trusts in him, and I am helped. My heart leaps for joy and I will give thanks to him in song.

The LORD is the strength of his people, a fortress of salvation for his anointed one. Save your people and bless your inheritance; be their shepherd and carry them forever.

Personal prayers for attacking the devil and putting on the whole armour of God

NINTH PRAYER.

Thanksgiving after being delivered from the spirit of death sent by your enemies

This prayer is taken from the book of *Psalm 9*. It is used during victory. Make sure after prayer you wait for the answer of what you prayed for and glorify Him. Do this with joy in your heart, smile and relax before God.

Psalms 9:1-10.
I will praise You, O Lord, with my whole heart; I will tell of all Your marvellous works.

I will be glad and rejoice in You; I will sing praise to Your name, O Most High.

When my enemies turn back, they shall fall and perish at Your presence. For You ,have maintained my right and my cause;

You sat on the throne judging in righteousness. You have rebuked the nations, You have destroyed the wicked; You have blotted out their name forever and ever. O enemy, destructions are finished forever!

And you have destroyed cities; Even their memory has perished. But the Lord shall endure forever; He has prepared His throne for judgment.

He shall judge the world in righteousness, And He shall administer judgment for the peoples in uprightness. The Lord also will be a refuge for the oppressed,

A refuge in times of trouble. And those who know Your name will put their trust in You; For You, Lord, have not forsaken those who seek You.

Personal prayers to destroy the power of witchcraft and magical powers

PRAYER ONE.

Fifteen prayers to destroy the evil spells

1   I destroy all the secret ideas of the enemy to bring misunderstanding among my family, by the blood of Jesus. Let my family be united and the evil plans of the enemy perish.

2   I destroy the secret plans of the wicked people sent to kill me, by the blood of Jesus. May the Lord let the spirit of death go back to destroy the sender, in Jesus' name.

3   I destroy all witches watching and sending spells on me, by the blood of

Jesus. May the power of spells die and never resurrect again forever.

4   I destroy all the evil spells being pronounced against me by the wicked people, by the blood of Jesus. May those spells be confused and return to destroy the sender. May the Lord bless me abundantly until my enemies fear me because of my wealth.

5   I destroy all the witchcraft power being sent to bring poverty to my life, by the blood of Jesus.

6   I destroy all the charms and witchcraft powers that are planning to attack me, by the blood of Jesus. Let those charms receive fire from the Lord and consume their powers.

7   I destroy the stronghold and all powers of the devil directed to attack me, by the blood of Jesus. Let those powers be defeated and get confused in Jesus' name.

8   I destroy all powers and plans of wicked spirits which are killing my family, by the blood of Jesus. May the Lord send them back where they came from and let the Lord protect my family from death.

9   I destroy all demonic powers that witches have sent from far to attack me, by the blood of Jesus. May those demonic powers be <u>destroyed</u> before they reach me. Let them die, in Jesus' name.

10   I destroy all powers of evil being sent by my relatives out of jealousy against my progress, by the blood of Jesus. May the Lord have mercy upon me and lift me higher than those who attack me, in Jesus' name.

11   I destroy the assignment of satanic spirits sent to attack my life, by the blood of Jesus. Let satanic spirits be

confused and go to hell. Let them perish. Let them die in Jesus' name.

12 I destroy all demonic powers that steal money out of my hands, by the blood of Jesus. May the Lord bless the work of my hands and help me manage my finances.

13 I destroy all spirits that have stolen my joy, by the blood of Jesus. Let the joy of the Lord be my strength.

14 I destroy all the wicked powers, always crawling in my bed to sleep with me and those that visit me in dreams, by the blood of Jesus. Let them not visit my room again. Let the Holy Spirit control the whole of my dwelling place.

15 I destroy all the bad dreams affecting my sleep, by the blood of Jesus. May the spirits controlling those dreams die before they reach my room. Let them perish before they sleep with me, in Jesus' name.

Personal prayers to destroy the power of witchcraft and magic power

SECOND PRAYER.

Prayer against the wickedness of man

Psalms 36: 1-4;
An oracle is within my heart concerning the sinfulness of the wicked:

There is no fear of God before his eyes. For in his own eyes he flatters himself too much to detect or hate his sin.

The words of his mouth are wicked and deceitful; he has ceased to be wise and to do good. Even on his bed he plots evil; he commits himself to a sinful course and does not reject what is wrong.'

May their evil plans go back to them.

May their wicked speeches and lies turn back to them and destroy them.

May their evil plans as they lie in bed work against them.

May their pride vanish and the glory of God defeat them.

Oh Lord! Let your kingdom rule forever.

May they be rewarded with the evil that they have done to people.

May their wickedness be confused and not succeed in Jesus' name.

**Personal prayers to destroy the power
of witchcraft and magic powers**

THIRD PRAYER.

Prayers against demonic attacks

May the Lord protect me day and night against evil people who plot against me.
May the Lord protect me from the spirits that attack day and night.
May the Lord send any spirit which attacks me back to the sender.

May the Lord hear my prayers and keep me safe from all attacks in this world.
Father you are the creator of the universe, the devil rebelled against you and you cast him out, with all the angels that supported him.
From your heavenly place, I am your child through your Son, Jesus Christ. But I feel the attacks of the enemy in my room at

nights. I hear voices, which do not belong to me.

Jehovah God, I pour out my heart to you. I seek your protection that the devourer, the accuser of the brethren, the liar, the murderer, the failure, the deceiver, shall not attack me, whether by witchcraft or by any other evil powers because Jehovah my God is in control of my dwelling.

Let the fire of the Holy Ghost come down now and destroy the spirits of the devil that are attacking me. You dangerous spirits, you do not belong to me.

I come against you in the name of Jesus. I destroy you in the name of Jesus.

It is over in the name of Jesus.

I am free from every demonic attack in the name of Jesus.

I am cleansed from the crown of my head to the soles of my feet, by the blood of Jesus.

Praise be to my Saviour.

Praise be to my deliverer.

The voices of spirits that attack my mind and witches' powers, I destroy you by the blood of Jesus.

In Jesus' name I am free. I have authority over you.

In Jesus' name, I say goodbye now to the evil spirits that were sent to attack me, in Jesus' name.

I come against any spirits sent by my enemies to kill me, in the name of Jesus.

I come against all evil spirits, which follow me everywhere I go, in the name of Jesus.

I come against all the evil powers that follow me because of the sins of my grand-parents, in the name of Jesus. I come against the spirit of death that attacks me with sickness, in the name of Jesus.

I render powerless all the spirits of witch-craft against my life, in the name of Jesus. I render powerless demonic forces from the kingdom of the devil following people in the day and at night, in the name of Jesus.

I render powerless the spirits of my ancestors that are following me, in the name of Jesus.

I render powerless every evil spirit of the dead people in my family that are causing problems to the community, in Jesus' name. I render powerless evil spirits sent by my relatives to destroy me in the name of Jesus. I render powerless any attack raised against me and sent to my place of work, in the name of Jesus.

I render powerless any spirits sent to me by the power of the devil to destroy my job, in the name of Jesus. Amen

**Personal prayers to destroy the power
of witchcraft and magic power**

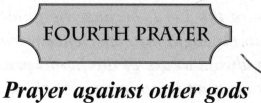

FOURTH PRAYER

Prayer against other gods

This prayer is taken from the Book of ***Psalm 16.*** It is for separating you from the sins of other gods and devil worshippers.

Psalms 16: 1-11.
Protect me, O God; I trust in you for safety.
I say to the Lord, "You are my Lord; all the good things I have come from you."
How excellent are the Lord's faithful people! My greatest pleasure is to be with them.
Those who rush to other gods bring many troubles on themselves.I will not take part in their sacrifices; I will not worship their gods.
You, Lord, are all I have, and you give me

all I need; my future is in your hands.
How wonderful are your gifts to me; how
good they are!
I praise the Lord, because he guides me,
and in the night my conscience warns me.
I am always aware of the Lord's presence;
he is near, and nothing can shake me.

And so I am thankful and glad, and I feel
completely secure, because you protect me
from the power of death. I have served you
faithfully, and you will not abandon me to
the world of the dead.

You will show me the path that leads to life;
your presence fills me with joy and brings
me pleasure forever.

**Personal prayers to destroy the power
of witchcraft and magic powers**

FIFTH PRAYER.

Eleven prayers to destroy witches power used to control your mind

1. I destroy anything the witches use as a point of contact to destroy marriages, by the blood of Jesus. May the Lord cover my life and protect me in my marriage.

2. I destroy all evil powers, affecting my eyes, my feet, my arms and my private parts, by the blood of Jesus. May the Lord anoint all my body and give me wisdom and knowledge to overcome temptation.

3. I destroy the powers that the witches use to control people's minds, by the blood of Jesus. Let the witches' plans be destroyed continually every day and night.

4 I destroy every assignment of the witches from the East to West and from South to North, by the blood of Jesus. Let all their evil assignments planned against me be confused and terminated by the Holy Spirit.

5 I destroy all their secret meetings being held in secret places, by the blood of Jesus. May the Holy Spirit reveal their evil plans and send fire to destroy them.

6 I destroy the spirit of death sent to kill people, by the blood of Jesus. May the Lord let the spirit of death return to the wicked people who have send them and destroy the sender.

7 I destroy every spell the witches have used to put sickness on people, by the blood of Jesus. Let all those spells sent be powerless and die before they affect people.

8   I destroy all spells that have already been cast to kill people, by the blood of Jesus. May the Lord destroy those spells with fire. Let them die, die in Jesus' name.

9   I destroy the evil spirit of death used by the witches to haunt people, by the blood of Jesus. May the Holy Spirit hunt and destroy them before they accomplish their mission.

10 I destroy the works of the spirit of infirmity that has been released by the devil to create sickness, by the blood of Jesus. May the power of sickness die before they reach people.

11 I destroy any plans of the wicked for the destruction of people, by the blood of Jesus. Let their plans be known to the Holy Spirit and be destroyed in Jesus' name.

Prayers to destroy the powers that cause sexual immorality & family destruction

FIRST PRAYER

Prayers against the spirit of lust

May the spirit of lust in my body, confusing my mind to have sex, stop now in the name of Jesus. May the demonic power enticing my body stop now.

May the spirit of lust die from my body. May the spirit of lust from the generation of my family die now. May the spirit of lust received from my grandparents die now.

May the spirits of the devil that seek to control the mind, body and soul die before they confuse me. May the Lord destroy all thoughts in my mind that lead me to do evil. May the Lord's grace and favour be upon me.

May the Lord have mercy upon me and protect me from the spirit of lust. May the Lord set the fire of the Holy Spirit against all evil spiritual attacks upon me.

May the Lord lift me above all my enemies and deliver me from the spirit of lust. May the Lord put my enemies to shame and not allow people to seduce me to have ungodly sex.

May the Lord destroy all evil that come to me through people leading me to lust. May the Lord protect my mind, my body, my pillow and my blanket not to allow any evil thoughts to confuse me, in the name of Jesus. Amen.

In the name of Jesus Christ, the Son of the living God, I come against the spirit of lust in my life that causes me to sin, by the blood of Jesus.

I declare war against the spirit of lust. You are from hell and I send you back to hell by the blood of Jesus, by the blood of Jesus,by the blood of Jesus. Amen!

May the Lord cleanse my body, my reproductive system, by the power and anointing of the Holy Spirit.

Now my body, you are dead in Christ and resurrected with Christ. I divorce the evil spiritual partners that cause me to desire ungodly sexual relationships.

I am free. I am free. Jesus has set me free through His blood, His precious and anointed blood. The pure blood is being applied to my sinful life now, in Jesus' name. Amen, Amen, Hallelujah, Hallelujah. Glory be to Jesus. Amen.

Prayers to destroy the powers that cause sexual immorality & family destruction

SECOND PRAYER.

Prayer for men and women, who, in their dreams, have sex with people

May God Jehovah, who created the heaven and the earth, God who made me in His own image, through Jesus Christ destroys the spiritual husband/wife coming to me in the night.

He blows the winds in all directions according to His will.

He made Adam and Eve, man and woman. I am tired of being married to a spiritual husband/wife and defiling my bed at night.

The blood of Jesus is against the evil spiritual partners.

You spirit of the enemy, spirit of confusion and destruction, you are in danger because I discover you do not belong to me.

You must come to an end. You must stop and go to hell. Don't touch me again. I am the temple of God, the Father, the Son and the Holy Spirit who is in me, and is very powerful. This is fire against you Amen.

Thank you my Lord, my Saviour, for destroying this spiritual husband/wife from my bed.

Glory be to Jesus my Saviour. May all the evil spirits coming to my bed die. May the spirit of sex in the dreams die.
May all my enemies in the spiritual realm die. May the power of spiritual partners die. May all the evil spirits sent by my enemies die.
The spirits of the dead, who are visiting me in the dream and having sex with me, may they be consumed by the fire of the Holy

Spirit now. May all the spirits of homosexuality and lesbianism, going around confusing people, not touch any of my family.

May the Holy Spirit confuse all the plans of the enemy raised against me in the dreams. May any person who sends evil spirits to sleep with me be blind. May anybody who admires me through evil, sexual lust perish now.

May any eye sending evil spirits in the day or in the night to have sex with me be blind. I destroy every spiritual husband/wife that controls my bed, by the blood of Jesus. I destroy the spirit of lust that makes my body desire unwanted sex.

May my body, which is the temple of God, stay holy by the help of God. My body shall be cleansed by the power of the Holy Spirit. May the Lord God lead me, guide me, help and protect me from evil sex, in Jesus' name. Amen.

Prayer to destroy the powers that cause sexual immorality & family destruction

THIRD PRAYER

Fifteen prayers to destroy the works of the devil causing attacks in the dreams

1   I destroy all evil plans to attack me in my dreams, by the blood of Jesus. May the Lord protect and keep me from dreaming things from the devil.

2   I destroy all bad dreams sent to me by witchcraft, by the blood of Jesus. Let the witches who send the dreams perish and not send any more bad dreams in Jesus' name.

3   I destroy the confusion brought in my life by the blood of Jesus. Let all bad dreams go back where they come from

and perish. They should not visit my house any more.

4   I destroy all powers that move my spirit in my dreams to different places, by the blood of Jesus. Lord, let them stop manipulating me in the dream. Let them die and not come again into my bed.

5.   I destroy all secrets of the devil that bring bad dreams to me, by the blood of Jesus. Let their secret plans be revealed and destroyed by the Holy Spirit, in Jesus' name.

6.   I destroy the powers behind dangerous dreams that are assigned presently to attack me in my sleep, by the blood of Jesus. May the Lord let all my sleep be comfortable and let the Holy Spirit cover me always when I am asleep.

7.   I destroy all the dangerous dreams channelled to my family, by the blood of Jesus. May the Lord let all my family

have comfortable sleep every night and may every evil plan and nightmares die before they come to us.

8. I destroy all dangerous dreams, which the enemy has assigned to come to me in the future, by the blood of Jesus. May those evil spirits that send heart attacks die before they reach my house.

9. I destroy any spirit sent to attack people while they are asleep by the blood of Jesus.

10. I destroy the powers of the spirit sent to bring heart attacks, which affect people at night when they are sleeping, by the blood of Jesus.

11. I destroy all the influencing spirits that control people even at night, by the blood of Jesus. Let those spirits die! die! die!, let them perish! perish! before they reach me.

12. I destroy the power of the spirit of the devil that influences me to do bad things, by the blood of Jesus. May the Lord destroy the influencing power and let the Holy Spirit confuse them.

13. I destroy the spirit of hatred sent by witches to make people hate me, by the blood of Jesus. May the Lord bless me and connect me with people who will love me forever instead of them hating me.

14. I destroy all the minds of witches planning evil against other people, by the blood of Jesus. May the blood of the lamb defeat them.

15. I destroy all evil plans before they are sent out to destroy people, by the blood of Jesus. Let these plans be confused and their mission be destroyed before they reach people.

Prayer to destroy the powers that cause sexual immorality& family destruction

FOURTH PRAYER.

Prayers to <u>destroy</u> attacks in marriages

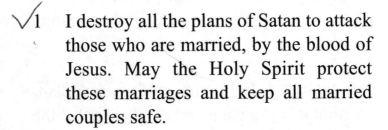

1   I destroy all the plans of Satan to attack those who are married, by the blood of Jesus. May the Holy Spirit protect these marriages and keep all married couples safe.

2   I destroy all witches powers used to snatch other people's partners, by the blood of Jesus. Lord let those who use them become blind.

3   I destroy the spirits that women use to confuse men, by the blood of Jesus. Let the eyes of those women be blind. Let them not destroy men by their evil

plans. May the Lord have mercy upon these men and open their minds and understanding for them to know good and bad.

4   I destroy any spirit that has been assigned to cause problems to those who are married, by the blood of Jesus. Let those spirits not enter any marriage, let them die! die! in Jesus' name.

5   I destroy all the ideas of the witches being planned to break marriages, by the blood of Jesus. May the Lord let those evil ideas perish before they spoil marriages.

6   I destroy any spell, evil power that is working in people's marriages to separate them, by the blood of Jesus. May the Lord protect those who are married and give them peace and unity.

7   I destroy all the evil powers, planned and sent by witches to confuse people not to get married, by the blood of Jesus.

8 I destroy all the evil eyes, which see people and put spells on them, by the blood of Jesus. May the Holy Spirit break those spells and set me free in Jesus' name.

10 I destroy any assignment of the wicked people against me, to create problems in my marriage, by the blood of Jesus. My marriage stands on the rock, which is Jesus Christ, and anybody who tries to cause problems must die.

11 I destroy all fear that come upon me to give chances to witches to destroy me, by the blood of Jesus. My marriage stands on the rock, which is Jesus Christ, and anybody who tries to cause problems must die.

12 I destroy the spirit of singleness that is assigned to affect my family, by the wicked people, by the blood of Jesus. Let the anointing of the Holy Spirit take control and overcome the spirit of singleness, in Jesus' name. Amen.

**Personal prayers to spec'
problems in your life**

FIRST PRAYER.

Prayer when your problems are overwhelming you

This prayer is taken from **Psalms 142**, it is to be used daily when you are experiencing unbearable situations and circumstances.

Psalms 142:1-7
I call to the Lord for help; I plead with him.

I bring him all my complaints; I tell him all my troubles.

When I am ready to give up, he knows what I should do. In the path where I walk, my enemies have hidden a trap for me.

When I look beside me, I see that there is no one to help me, no one to protect me. No one cares for me.

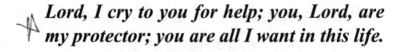

Lord, I cry to you for help; you, Lord, are my protector; you are all I want in this life.

Listen to my cry for help, for I am sunk in despair. Save me from my enemies; they are too strong for me.

Set me free from my distress; then in the assembly of your people I will praise you because of your goodness to me.

Personal prayers to specific problems in your life

SECOND PRAYER.

Prayer for forgiveness of sins and errors of your youth

This prayer is taken from the book of **Psalm 25** and will set you free from destruction because of your past sins.

Psalms 25:1-22
To you, O Lord, I offer my prayer; in you, my God, I trust. Save me from the shame of defeat; don't let my enemies gloat over me!

Defeat does not come to those who trust in you, but to those who are quick to rebel against you.

Teach me your ways, O Lord; make them known to me.

Teach me to live according to your truth, for you are my God, who saves me. I always trust in you.

Remember, O Lord, your kindness and constant love which you have shown from long ago.

Forgive the sins and errors of my youth. In your constant love and goodness, remember me, Lord!

Because the Lord is righteous and good, he teaches sinners the path they should follow.

He leads the humble in the right way and teaches them his will.

With faithfulness and love he leads all who keep his covenant and obey his commands.

Keep your promise, Lord, and forgive my sins, for they are many.

Those who have reverence for the Lord will learn from him the path they should follow.

They will always be prosperous, and their children will possess the land.

The Lord is the friend of those who obey him and he affirms his covenant with them.

I look to the Lord for help at all times, and he rescues me from danger.

Turn to me, Lord, and be merciful to me, because I am lonely and weak.

Relieve me of my worries and save me from all my troubles.

Consider my distress and suffering and forgive all my sins.

See how many enemies I have; see how much they hate me.

Protect me and save me; keep me from defeat. I come to you for safety.

May my goodness and honesty preserve me, because I trust in you.

From all their troubles, O God, save your people Israel!

Personal prayers to specific problems in your life

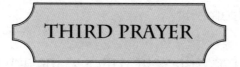

THIRD PRAYER

Prayer for a widow/widower

Father God, I am lonely because I lost my husband/wife. He/she has died and I find myself a widow/widower. I pour my heart out to you. I cry to you for help.

My partner has gone and I am left with emptiness. There is a gap in my life father God.
I miss my partner, that is why I always put my trust in you. You care and look after the helpless. Your love is like a river that flows from the mountain to the lowest valley.

You provide food for the birds because you love them. I trust you for my daily bread, for my budget, my house, my bills, my transport and my clothes. I need you all the time, I need you everyday, I need you O God. Jehovah God, remember me. Do not turn away from me.

Cover me with your wings as the hen covers its chicks. I trust in you, in Jesus' name. I know through you I will be happy. Let your blessings overshadow me, in Jesus' name. Amen.

Personal prayers to specific problems in your life

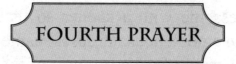

FOURTH PRAYER

Prayer for those who are homeless

Father God I am homeless.

I have nowhere to put my head.

The world has turned against me.

No matter what I do, I find I am still helpless.

The devil is destroying my life with the spirit of lack.

Lord, I want to be obedient to you.

I dismantle the works of this spirit of darkness that is tormenting me and making me to be homeless.

I come to you, God the father, God the Son and God the Holy Spirit.

Purify me, cleanse me and change me.

Touch me and bless me with accommodation.

Open doors for me so I can also rejoice because you love people like me.

Let your mighty hand and mercy touch me and bless me with a shelter so that I can dwell in a good house in Jesus' name. Spirit of lack, spirit of poverty, spirit of the devil. I come against you in the name of Jesus. You must leave me now and go.

I do not belong to you. I claim my blessing from God. I possess good accommodation, in Jesus' name. Satan, enough is enough. I will never stay homeless because Jesus loves me. He died for me and He cares for me.

He delivers me from the hands of Satan. Satan your wicked power over my life has come to an end

In Jesus' name I am free from every bondage. Amen.

Hallelujah! Glory be to Jesus. The Lord of Lords. Amen!

**Personal prayers to specific
problems in your life**

FIFTH PRAYER.

*Prayer against high blood
pressure and diabetes*

Heavenly father I come to you in the name
of Jesus. I have been diagnosed with high
blood pressure and diabetes. These are
dangerous sicknesses that have terminated
many people's lives.

*Isaiah 53:5"But because of our sins He
was wounded, beaten because of the evil
we did. We are healed by the punishment
he suffered, made whole by the blows he
received."*
I confess that I have been made whole. I am
healed from <u>high blood pressure</u> and
<u>diabetes.</u>
I come against the spirits causing this

deadly sickness that I might have inherited from my parents and grand parents.

High blood pressure and diabetes, there is no room for you in my body. I overcome you by the blood of Jesus.
Through His blood, my blood is cleansed, purified, sanctified in the name of Jesus. In Jesus' name I am <u>healed.</u>
The bible says, **'let the weak say , I am strong.'**

I confess that I am healed from high blood pressure and diabetes. Jesus surround me with your blessings, grace and good health. Hallelujah! Hallelujah! I am <u>healed</u> in Jesus' name. Amen.

**Personal prayers to specific
problems in your life**

SIXTH PRAYER

*Prayer when going
for a job interview*

Father God, your promise with Abraham is
coming to pass in my life, through this interview.

You promise blessings and I am facing an
interview for me to earn an income through
the work of my hands.

I know that some people are against my
success. Even the devil is not happy if I
succeed.

Let the principalities and powers that can
come against this opportunity which you
have given to me perish now in Jesus' name.

You wicked spirits that are trying to hinder this interview, I nullify your powers. I dismantle your forces.

I send confusion to you by the Holy Spirit. You will never , never put your hand on my job.

I send the Holy Spirit in advance, to control every situation. I send fire to nullify and dismantle the spirit of fear in the name of Jesus. I cover myself by the blood of Jesus. Lord, by your heavenly power make me to be bold and wise in the interview, in Jesus' name.

I have victory and confess that the job is mine.

I have it.

I possess it,

I receive it,

In Jesus' name.

Amen.

Personal prayers to specific problems in your life

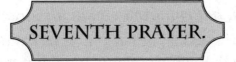

SEVENTH PRAYER.

Prayer when you are about to be sacked

The Heaven and the earth are for you God. You made the mountains, the oceans and the earth. All things belong to you O God.

Deuteronomy 28:2
"Obey the Lord your God and all these blessings will be yours.'

According to the word O God, my work is a blessing and no power of the enemy can come against my work in Jesus' name."

Deuteronomy 28: 7

'The Lord will defeat your enemies when they attack you. They will attack from onedirection, but run from you in all directions.'

I know that whosoever is touching my job is rising against me.
According to your word, they shall flee from me.

They must flee from me in Jesus' name. I possess my job.

I possess my job.
I possess my job in Jesus' name.
I send terror, confusion to every evil spirit working against my job.

I send fire to every works of the enemy against my job in Jesus' name.

I claim my promotion.
I possess my promotion.
I have my promotion in Jesus' name. Amen.

I have it.
I have it.

I receive my promotion now in Jesus' name. Holy Ghost, move in my workplace. Father let your favour be upon me 24hrs and your protection be upon me 24hrs in Jesus' name. Amen.

Personal prayers to specific problems in your life

EIGHTH PRAYER.

Protection from the snares of evildoers

This prayer is taken from the book of **Psalms 141** and is for protection against the evil people who want to harm you.

Psalm 141: 1-10.

1   O Lord, I call to you; come to me quickly; hear my voice when I cry to you.

2   Let my prayer rise before you as incense the lifting up of my hands as the evening sacrifice.

3   **Set a watch before my mouth, O Lord, and guard the door of my lips;**

4   **Let not my heart incline to any evil thing; let me not be occupied in wickedness with evil doers, nor taste the pleasures of their table.**

5   **Let the righteous smite me in a friendly way; but let not the oil of the unrighteous anoint my head; my prayer is continually against their wicked deeds.**

6   **Let the wicked rulers be overthrown in stony places; then they may know that my words are sweet.**

7   **As when a plough turns over the earth in furrows, let their bones be scattered at the mouth of the Pit.**

8   *But my eyes are turned to you, Lord God; in you I take refuge; do not leave me defenceless.*

9   *Protect me from the snare which they have laid for me and from the traps of the evil doers.*

10 *Let the wicked caught into their own nets, while I pass by in safety.*

Personal prayers to specific problems in your life

NINTH PRAYER.

Prayers for guidance and protection from any defeat

This prayer is taken from the book of Psalms 25 to be used daily for seeking God's protection.

Psalm 25: 1-7
To you, O LORD, I lift up my soul.

I trust in you, my God! Do not let me be disgraced, or let my enemies rejoice in my defeat. No one who trusts in you will ever be disgraced, but disgrace comes to those who try to deceive others.

Show me the path where I should walk, O LORD; point out the right road for me to follow.Lead me by your truth and teach me, for you are the God who saves me. All day long I put my hope in you.

Remember, O LORD, your unfailing love and compassion, which you have shown from long ages past. Forgive the rebellious sins of my youth; look instead through the eyes of your unfailing love, for you are merciful, O LORD.

Prayer for rebuking Satan

Mark 9:25: 'Jesus noticed that the crowd was closing in on them, so He gave a command to the evil spirit. Deaf and dumb spirit, He said. I order you to come out of the boy and never go into him again.'

As Jesus rebuked Satan who attacks me at night, and attacks people in the day time, so I confess today, that I am covered by the blood of Jesus.

And I rebuke Satan.
I rebuke evil spirits.
I rebuke the spirit of witchcraft in the name of Jesus.
The spirit of the evil, the spirit of poverty, I rebuke you, in the name of Jesus. I rebuke you, in the name of Jesus.
I cast you out, in the name of Jesus.
I cast you out , in the name of Jesus.

I invite the Holy Spirit into my life, and I cover myself with the blood of Jesus and the power of the Holy Spirit.

In the name of Jesus, Satan you will never enter into me.

Because the blood of Jesus covers me 24 hours a day.

You will never enter into my family, nor in my life anymore, in Jesus' name. Amen.

Prayer for overcoming the power of Satan

In the name that is above all names, in the name of Jesus Christ, I have been given power to tread over serpents and scorpions, and over all the power of the enemy , by any means nothing shall hurt me.

Luke 10:19.
'Listen I have given you authority, so that you can walk on snakes and scorpions and overcome all the power of the enemy, and nothing will hurt you.'

Now in the name of Jesus Christ, I have been given power to render Satan is power-less, in Jesus' name. I apply, apply and apply the blood of Jesus to my life.
I apply, apply and apply the blood of Jesus to my house.
I apply, apply and apply the blood of Jesus to my family.

I apply and apply the blood of Jesus into my business.

I apply, apply the blood of Jesus into my finances.

I render all demons powerless. Satan you are under my feet.

Satan, you are under the soles of the feet of the believers. Satan you can do nothing against me in Jesus' name.

You are finished. Satan, your works are over. I am dangerous to you, because Jesus has given me power over you in His name.

Prayer for protection when enemies surround you

Psalms 109: 3-6
They have spoken against me with a lying tongue;
they encompassed me with words of hatred and fought against me without a cause.

In return for my love, they set themselves against me,
even though I had prayed for them.

Thus have they repaid me with evil for good,
and hatred for my good will.

Father, in the name of Jesus Christ,
My enemies are surrounding me,
They are everywhere,
Wherever I walk people are against me.
They speak lies, they bring confusion

against me.
They hate me.
I am lonely.
I have nobody to talk to.

But I give myself to prayer, Oh! Lord.
I believe that you will answer my prayer, by
the power of the Holy Spirit.
I come to you Oh! Lord,

And you judge because you are in charge.
You command me to do no evil to my
enemies. Forgive my sins and let my prayer
for forgiveness come to you.

Father, my enemies shall run away from me,
And I will never, never have regrets because
you are on my side, And I will never, ever
forget your Glory.
May your Glory come upon me.
may your Anointing come upon me.
may the Power of the Holy Spirit come
upon me everywhere I go
Let the Holy Spirit go ahead of me

and destroy every work of Satan.
Change my enemies, take Satan out of their
lives. Redeem them, give them salvation
and let my enemies become my friends.

Lord, I know that you are going to do it.
Let my father-in-law not be my enemy. Let
my mother-in-law, my sister-in-law, my
brother-in-law, my husband, my children
and all the people around me, not turn
against me.

Holy Spirit, keep peace between me and my
neighbours And the people around me.
In Jesus' name.
In Jesus' name.
In Jesus' name. Amen.
Glory be to Hosanna the Most High God.
Amen.

Prayer against Satan and the people interfering with your marriage

Father in the name of Jesus Christ, I come to you through the Holy Spirit.
I come to you under the anointing of the Holy Spirit.
I come to you in prayer now. Hear my voice.
My prayer shall come to your holy dwelling place in heaven.

According to the book of *Psalms 27:1*
The LORD is my light and my salvation; whom shall I fear?

The LORD is the strength of my life; of whom shall I be afraid?

King of kings, Son of the living God,
People are coming against my marriage.
A woman is interfering with my marriage

(mention her name). JB -
A man is interfering with my marriage (mention his name).
My marriage is being destroyed by Satan. Satan wants to separate me from my beloved wife/husband. —
Now in the name of Jesus Christ, the name above all names, I speak victory. I speak authority. I speak anointing. —
I cast out evil spirits that want to separate me from my beloved one, my partner (mention the name of your partner). RW

In the name of Jesus Christ
My enemy who is interfering in my marriage,
I send fire of the Holy Spirit to destroy you Satan in Jesus' name.
Holy Ghost take control
In the name of Jesus.
Let all the spirit of witchcraft
That has been sent to destroy my marriage
Be blinded in Jesus' name.
In Jesus' name,
In Jesus' name.

I call upon the Holy Spirit to come now.

In Jesus' name I pray.

In Jesus' name I pray.

Holy Spirit, welcome, welcome, welcome.

✓ Welcome into my room.

✓ Welcome into my bedroom.

✓ Welcome into my dwelling place.

I cover my partner with the blood of Jesus.

I remove my partner from the work of the evil spirits.

I bring my partner to the glory of God in Jesus' name.

Amen.

Prayer when you are going to bed at night

Father in the name of Jesus Christ,
It has become dark, from day light to darkness. I am going to bed.
The devil walks in the darkness.
Satan moves at night.
Satan brings problems at night
But as I am going to my bed,
I want my peace to be in my bed.
I want to have a nice sleep.
Every evil spirit that attacks people at night, at anytime, in the name of Jesus,
You will never touch me again.
I apply the blood of Jesus in my bedroom.
I apply the blood of Jesus over me and my family. I apply the blood of Jesus into my house. I invite the Holy Spirit into every part of my dwelling place.
In the name of Jesus Christ, Holy Spirit, thank you for taking care of me through the night until morning, in Jesus' name.
Amen.

Prayer in the morning when you wake up

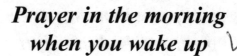

Father, it has turned from darkness to light.
I get out of bed, lifting my heart and my hands to you
Welcome the day which is a new day for me.
This day has come. I have never seen it,
Oh! God, but it is a day.
That I am going to walk through in victory
I come to you O Lord Almighty,
Because this day is going to be a day of blessing for me.
Let the Holy Spirit move with me this day.
All the plans that Satan has planned
Against me this day
Must be thwarted by the Holy Spirit.

Every dangerous weapon
That the devil has planned
Against me at my workplace,
Or wherever I go today,
I apply the Holy Spirit to destroy them all.

I apply the Holy Spirit on you devil.
I apply the Holy Spirit on you.
The Holy Spirit is fighting against you.
The Holy Spirit is destroying you
In the name of Jesus.
On behalf of my family and my life,
I present every need of mine to the Holy Spirit
And I dedicate this day to the
Holy Spirit in Jesus' name I pray. Amen.

Prayer when you are attending a family funeral

God the Father, the Son and the Holy Spirit,
You are a spirit, I am a spirit created by you.
And you dwell in me. I am your temple.
Now I am facing a funeral
Where people are doing rituals. They are also performing traditional rituals,
But Father, because I want to be on your side.
I want to be with you.
I want to be the way you want me to be.
Now, separate me from the things of the world.
The traditional rituals of the family that would make me offend your Holy Spirit.

Cover me with the Holy Spirit.
Walk with me to the home of the funeral.
Take care of my life, my lips, my mouth and my mind.
Don't let Satan trap me into
speaking evil.

Let Satan be defeated when I am at the funeral and every spirit of ritual, spirit of the dead, spirit of the danger, spirit of witchcraft, that can come to me during this funeral.

I send the fire of Holy Spirit to thwart, to destroy, dismantle your powers and I cover myself with the Holy Spirit.

Holy Spirit, cover me now at the time of this funeral.

Holy Spirit, cover me now at this difficult time because I know that with you all things are possible.

Holy Spirit, welcome.
Cover the burial place.
Cover everybody.
Cover my family,
Cover my father, cover
my mother. Cover my family in Jesus' name.Hallelujah!Hallelujah!

The glory and the power of the Lord be upon me during this day of the funeral and the peace of the Lord dwell in me, in Jesus' name.

Prayer when you are in financial difficulties

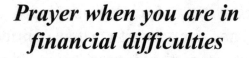

In the name that is above all names, the name of Jesus, the name that works miracles. The bible says in the book of ***Psalms 27:1***: ***"The Lord is my light and my salvation, whom shall I fear? The Lord is the strength of my life, of whom shall I be afraid?'***

Financial lack, I will not be afraid of you. The Lord is my shepherd and is my salvation. Now even though I do not have money in my bank account, in my hand, I know all things are God's and I believe that in God I am blessed no matter how tough things are. Today and from now onwards, I am receiving my blessings.

As the Bible says in Psalms 24:5: 'He shall receive the blessings from the Lord, and righteousness from the Lord of his salvation."

I am receiving the blessings of finance now. My salvation is in God and by the blood of

Jesus His Son,

I am a righteous person. I speak now, that the financial blessing is upon me. I speak to you money, come to me. I call upon the Holy Ghost to bring finances to me. I speak the anointing to bring money to me.

I believe and I trust in Jesus, in the name that is above all names. In the name of Jesus Christ, money in this world is mine. I possess it, I have it, I receive it now in my purse/wallet I speak that I have money in Jesus' name.

I cast out the spirit of lack. I will never lack again because God is going to bless me, in Jesus' name. Amen.

In the name that is above all names, in the name of Jesus,

I am blessed in the city. I am blessed in the field. I am blessed when I come in and when I go out. I am blessed.

I am blessed in the name of Jesus. The blessings of the Lord is upon me. Amen.

Prayer when the spirit of death is surrounding you

(Everyone of your family is facing death)

Psalms 33: 19; 'To deliver their souls from death and to keep them alive in famine.'

Father, I come to you in the name of Jesus Christ. Death has really taken most of my family,
I am left here, we are only a few left.

Everyone is passing away.
They passed away because maybe, our grandparents sinned
And we have really offended you.
I repent of the sins of my grandparents, my mother and my father,
Sins that enable Satan to destroy , kill and finish us.
In the name of Jesus Christ
Lord forgive me and save my soul.
Deliver me from death.
Deliver me from famine.

Deliver me from the problems that are facing the nations of the world Now take care of me, control me. King of kings, the Son of the living God,

Your blood is powerful. Now I apply your blood to my life And to the life of my family. Protect me, keep me alive. Let me see the days to come. I know the spirit of lack shall never be upon me.
I fear nothing because I know that you are covering me.

Now death stop.
You will never touch me.
You will never kill me.
You will never destroy me
Because the blood of Jesus is upon me.
I speak to death,
'Death you are finished.
You will never touch me.
I will fear you no more.
I take the shield of faith
And the anointing of the Holy Spirit
To cover me all the days of my life.

No premature death shall fall upon my life.
In Jesus' name. Amen.
I will fear no evil nor will I fear death
From today onwards,
I am redeemed of the Lord in Jesus' name.
Amen.

Prayer for the peace of Jerusalem

In the book of *Psalms 122:6*: *"The bible says that those people who are praying for the peace of Jerusalem shall prosper.'*

Father, I lift Jerusalem into your hands.
Let your Holy Spirit cover Jerusalem.
Let the nations who surround Jerusalem with weapons be destroyed, by the blood of Jesus. I cover Jerusalem with the anointing of the Holy Spirit.
Let the power of God change the community of Israel.
Let all the dwelling places of Jerusalem be blessed.

Peace, joy and the blessings,
Shall cover the wall of Jerusalem.
I call the blessing upon Jerusalem.
I call the Holy Ghost upon Jerusalem.
I call the anointing upon Jerusalem,
In the name of Jesus Christ.
Jerusalem shall prosper.

Jerusalem shall succeed.

Jerusalem shall overcome her enemies, in Jesus' name.

Let the walls of Jerusalem be covered by the anointing.

In the name of Jesus Christ,

Father I confess that Jerusalem is your nation and your city.

I am a city dweller.

Don't pass me by,

When you are blessing Jerusalem, bless me Oh! Lord. I seek your Holy Spirit. I seek your anointing, as a gentile

But you have changed me.

You have honoured me and because of the blood of Jesus,

I will not fear.

O God, when you are giving your blessings,

When you are remembering your city of Jerusalem, remember me.

Don't pass me by,

In Jesus' name. Hallelujah! Glory be to the King Jesus Christ, the Son of the living God, the King of Jerusalem.

The one who answers by fire,
I vow that I shall serve you all the days of
my life.

You are wonderful, you are our blessing.
You are wonderful, you are our blessing.
You are the over comer
In the name that is above all names.
Thank you Jesus.
 Thank you Emmanuel.

Prayer when you find yourself speaking to things you don't like

(The essence of this prayer is taken from **Psalms 120**).

Oh! Lord, I cry to you and I come to you the King of Kings.
Deliver my soul from lying lips and from deceitful tongues.
I give myself unto thee.

Oh! Lord, I have done evil
Because my tongue speaks things which I don't like,
It speaks false things.
It speaks words that sometimes may even destroy me.
Lord, give me understanding and victory so that I will be able to stand against the enemy
Who is using my lips to abuse
And to destroy people with my mouth.

My mouth, I cleanse you with the blood of Jesus.

I cover you with the anointing
As from today, in the name of Jesus Christ.
I want to speak only holy, holy things, holy words.

My mouth, I cover you.
My lips, I seal you.
In the name of Jesus Christ.
I cover you by the anointing of the Holy Spirit.
Speak things of heaven
Speak things of anointing.
Speak things of victory, in Jesus' name. Amen.
Holy Spirit welcome,
and change and destroy every work of the enemy.
Cover me with the blood of Jesus.
In Jesus' name I pray. Amen.

Command Satan out of the life of a person who has backslidden

Satan who makes people backslide,
I come to you in the name of Jesus Christ.
In the name of Jesus,
(mention the name) was born again,
And Satan you have taken him/her back again.
I call this woman/man
By the anointing of the Holy Spirit
To come back to the Lord and serve the Lord.

Satan, where are your works?
Your works are finished,
Completely finished.
Your works are perishing.
Your works are over.
Your works no longer exist.
In the name of Jesus Christ,
I come against you Satan.

Satan, you, you, you are finished.

Release this woman/man to come and serve the Lord.

I rebuke you in Jesus' name, come out of his/her life.

I call him/her to the anointing of the Holy Spirit.

Holy Spirit cover this woman/man.

Convict him/her to receive salvation and serve him/her from the works of the enemy, in Jesus' name. Amen.

Prayer when your children are disobedient to you

Lord Jehovah, God who created heaven and earth.
God who formed me,
God who knew me before I was born,
You brought me into this world.
My children are the fruits of my womb,
The fruits of my body.

My children are disobedient to me.
They are arrogant and they disobey me.
They don't want to know me,
But now I want to bring them to you God,
Jehovah
Because you can change
Their understanding and behaviour
So that they may follow your ways.
I pray for my children (mention their
names).
I pray for them and I bring them to you Oh!
God, hear me

Bring them back to the anointing of the Holy Spirit.
I pray for them and I bring them to you,
Oh! God, hear me as their parent.
Bring them back to the anointing of the Holy Spirit.
I pray for them and I bring them to you.
Oh! God hear me as their parent.
Bring them back to the anointing of the Holy Spirit.

I claim them for you.
I take them away from the hands of the devil
I bring them to your holy place and holy dwelling.
I overcome the work of the Satan in their lives.
I destroy the work of Satan by the blood of Jesus.
I apply the blood of Jesus in their lives.
I apply the blood of Jesus wherever they move.
I cover them now.
I send the Holy Spirit to arrest them and bring them to your glory.

Father, my children are my future.
What will I benefit if I live in this world
And later leave people who are arrogant,
Who are disobedient to the nation, to the people?
Father, hear my prayer.
I know you hear the prayer of parents.
This time I ask you to cover me with your anointing and let me overcome the works of Satan, in Jesus' name.

Holy Spirit, deliver my children from the works of Satan.

And bring them to the Glory of God, in Jesus' name.

Holy Spirit you are wonderful, As I send you, I know you will answer my prayer
Since you are my umbrella, my comforter.
Now my children, I put anointing upon you by faith in Jesus' name.
You must change to Christ.
You must change to goodness.

You must obey what I am saying
Because you are my children.
I am a child of God and the bible says you
have to respect me
And I have to respect God.
In the name of Jesus Christ I release you to
the Holy Spirit in Jesus' name. Amen.

Confession

Faith is to speak things that are coming to pass even though they are not yet there. Faith is a total.believe that what you are speaking is what God is going to do. Confession is to speak, admit and acknowledge things. As a Christian you must confess the positive. Don't confess the negative. Negative things are from the devil. Positive things are from God. As I am going to lead you in confession, I want you to understand that you are confessing things with your own mouth, they are coming to pass in your life.

We are going to confess using bible verses and to claim them. When you confess something, claim it. When you confess something that you need, take it. There is also confession of declaration. You declare war against Satan.

I am going to lead you in confession in this book. We have been seeing a lot of great changes that happen to people who confess positively, in Jesus' name.

Confession to be obedient to God

I confess today that I will be obedient to God.

And that I will keep all His commandments.

I confess today that I am born again.

I confess today that I overcome Satan.

I confess today that my name is written in the book of life, as mentioned in the bible.

In the name of Jesus Christ, No weapon that is formed against me shall prosper.

No evil that shall attack me shall prevail.

No witchcraft power that attacks me, shall overcome me.

I speak this in Jesus' name.

I confess it in Jesus' name.

I believe it in Jesus' name.

I trust in God now,

That this confession is done in Jesus' name.

God the Father, the Son and the Holy Spirit, thank you for taking care of me now and for the rest of my life.

In Jesus' name. Amen.

Confession to overcome Satan in your family

I confess today that because the blood of
Jesus Christ is upon me,
The whole of my family is covered.
I am ready to fight a good fight with Satan.
I confess that Satan will never overcome my
family.
I believe in the blood of Jesus Christ
And His resurrection.
I believe in the anointing of the Holy Spirit
which came upon the disciples on the day of
Pentecost.

I believe in the healing of Jesus Christ.
I confess that Satan is under my feet.
I confess again that Satan has no room in
my life.
In the life of my father,
In the life of my mother.
In the life of my children,
In the life of my family.
I confess with my mouth,

And I believe that Satan must bow.
In everything that I put my hand into.
I confess today that Jesus Christ is Lord and
Satan is a loser.

I believe that Satan has lost the battle
And that I have won the battle.
Now I confess, I believe, and I trust God
that nothing shall harm me
All the days of my life, in Jesus' name.

Confession to destroy Satan's power in your life

My body is the temple of God.
God the Father, the Son and the Holy Spirit
dwell in me. The anointing controls my life.
Now I confess in the name of Jesus Christ
that sickness, disease and all kinds of
infirmities will never be under my
dwellings. They must not stay in my body
Because my body is the temple of God.
I believe that my body is the temple of God
my partner, my children, are the temples of
God.
Satan you must understand from my confession that you have no room in my life.
Sickness (mention the sickness e.g. stomach
ache, fibroid, leg pain, AIDS disease) leave
my body now in Jesus' name.
I confess victory in the name of Jesus
Christ. Holy Spirit, thank you for being in
my confession.
Heal, cover and anoint my body in Jesus'
name.

Confessing all things of God are yours

John 16:15 *"All that the Father has is mine; this is what I mean when I say that the Spirit will reveal to you whatever he receives from me."*

I confess that all things that Jesus has are mine.
I confess that the things of God are mine.
Everything I need in this world is mine.

In the name of Jesus Christ,
All good things of God are mine.
Praise be to Hosanna.

Praise be to Emmanuel. Praise be to Jesus. I overcome Satan by the blood of the Lamb.
Glory! Glory! Glory!
Glory! Glory! Glory!
Glory be to Jesus in His name. Amen.

Holy Spirit, the glory of God.

The spirit of truth comes upon me.

The spirit of truth guide me.

The spirit of truth speaks on my behalf.

Because whatever you speak is being answered by God, and you will show me great things.

Spirit of truth, spirit of blessing, spirit of holiness, I come to you as a humble servant of God.

I come to you as a sinner.

Welcome into my situation.

Dwell in my dwelling place.

Dwell in my presence.

Show me how to pray.

Glory be to the One who made the world.

And destroy Satan's power in Jesus' name.

Speaking to the Holy Spirit

Holy Spirit I feel your presence upon me.
Holy Spirit I need to speak with you all the time.
Holy Spirit I sleep with you.
I wake up with you.
I walk with you.
Thank you for filling me again.
Thank you, thank you, Holy Spirit.
Thank you, thank you again.
I am holy because you are in me.
Let your power continue dwelling within me.
Holy Spirit break every power of darkness.
Holy Spirit you are mine.
And I feel you.
Let your presence cover me twenty-four hours a day
In Jesus' name.

The enemies in danger

Exodus 23:22: 'But if you obey him and do everything I command, I will fight against all your enemies.'

I confess this today that God is my God. I confess today that what the bible says about me, God will bring it to come to pass. God has heard me, now my enemies are in danger. God is against them all.

All the enemies who come to me through witches, all the enemies coming to me by the power of the evil one, in the name of Jesus, I confess that I have victory over all of them. I have power, I have authority, I have overcome you by the blood of Jesus Christ.

Now I declare war against my enemies. I send the Holy Spirit to attack them. Evil spirits will not attack me. I have power to attack them because the Holy Spirit is in me.

There is a power greater than all the power of darkness. This is the power of the Holy Spirit. Now in the name of Jesus, all my enemies must vanish in Jesus' name.

The Lord's protection

***Exodus 13:21**: 'And the Lord went before them by day in a pillar of cloud to lead the way, and by night in a pillar of fire to give them light to go by day and night.'*

God Jehovah. God of Israel, God of Moses, God who move mountains from His people's lives.

You did wonders for Moses in the wilderness. Now I confess that, just as you led the people of Israel by day by a cloud and at night by a pillar of fire, so now I am being led by the Holy Spirit. As you walked with them day and night, so the Holy Ghost is walking with me day and night. I know Lord, that you love me. I want to confess that you are my God.

I will not serve any other god besides you. As I serve you, Satan is in danger. Satan, I want you to know that I belong to Jesus. As I belong to Jesus, you are in danger.

Now I call the name of Jesus against you Satan.

You must vanish from my family.
You must vanish from my finances.
You must vanish from my everything I put my hand to, because God is my God. He loves me and I will remain His forever, in Jesus' name.

God's favour

Exodus 3:21 "I will make the Egyptians respect you so that when my people leave they will not go empty- handed"

I confess that God has given me favour.
And wherever I go I shall not leave empty handed.
I confess that the prosperity of this world is mine.
I confess that good houses in this world are mine.
I confess that food in this world is mine.
I confess that things that are good in this world are mine.
Because God said He would have favour upon the people of Israel.
Now I am favoured because of the Holy Spirit in me.

Now I confess victory,
I confess success.

I confess that every good thing in this world is mine.

Satan, I declare war against you.

You must know that I am favoured by God.

And because I am favoured by God, you must stop harassing my finances.

You must stop bringing sicknesses into my body.

You are defeated in Jesus' name.

Satan, I overcome you.

Satan, I conquer you.

Satan, I overpower you, in Jesus' name.

Holy Spirit, I trust in you.

Every problem in this world shall never overcome me.

Because our God is Jehovah Jireh.

Let God who answers by fire be my God in Jesus' name. Amen.

Receiving what you ask for

John 16:23; *"Verily, verily I say unto you whatsoever you shall ask in the name of the Father, He shall give unto you."*

The Bible says that whatsoever I shall ask the Father, in the name of Jesus Christ, it shall be given unto me.
I claim a financial miracle.
I claim my permanent healing.
I claim victory. I claim power to overcome Satan.
All Satan's power must bow.
Evil spirits must bow in Jesus' name.
Satan, I overcome you.
And whatever, I ask in the name of Jesus Christ.
I have it forever in His name Amen.

Holy Spirit take control.
Holy Spirit, Holy Spirit,
Holy Spirit, anoint me again.

Holy Spirit, Holy Spirit,
Holy Spirit, you make me so happy.
You are my beloved.
You are my comforter.
You are my guide.
Because you are in me, Holy Spirit,
Everything I ask, I receive it in Jesus' name.
Glory be to Jesus, Emmanuel, God with us.
Glory be to the one who resurrected.
Hallelujah! Glory be to Jesus the Most High
God.
In your name Lord, I pray. Amen.

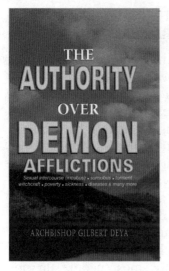

THE AUTHORITY OVER DEMON AFFLICTIONS

In modern times, many people are not aware of the main force behind endless human suffering and afflictions such as incurable diseases, witchcraft, unexplained deaths, curses, calamities, hatred, uncontrollable circumstances, job losses, financial troubles such as the credit crunch, and juvenile delinquencies among others.

Archbishop Gilbert Deya in his book, 'The Authority Over Demon Afflictions', clearly narrates the causes of such problems and demonstrates what it means 'living under Belzebub', the ruler of demons. He describes the origin of demons and demonstrates that the authority and commission to cast out demons still exists today. He challenges the reader to make the decision to examine their circumstances and to seek appropriate guidance on how to be in control of their life.

EXTRAORDINARY MIRACLES FOR YOU

Many people in modern times are faced with difficulties and challenges such as diseases that rule their lives causing them to be helpless. Extraordinary Miracles For You by Archbishop Gilbert Deya is a book that creates an atmosphere for those in need of the healing touch of Jesus Christ. The Archbishop writes "Even today, most people do not recognise that Jesus is still performing miracles".

In this book, you will find:

- Diseases render high profile helpless
- Unfortunate and the heroes perish
- Miracle healing by the Holy Communion
- Infirmities destroyed
- Faith works miracles
- Faith has made thee whole
- Miracle healing of a veteran soldier
- Sickness must be uprooted
- Miracle healing of the rotten hip bones

CLAIMING BACK YOUR INHERITANCE BY FORCE

Are faithful Christians aware of their rights of inheritance in Jesus' name. Can they forcefully take back what belongs to them? Archbishop Gilbert Deya has asked himself many times about the level of awareness and authority Christians have regarding the authority they should be taking to guarantee their inheritance. He has written in 'Claiming Back Your Inheritance By Force.' that all Christians who are the true believers have a destiny and by the power of the Holy Spirit and faith in God, they are qualified to possess the blessings of God at all costs, no matter what it takes...including use of force.

Many Christians are functioning below their expected levels and are therefore victims of disappointment and loss. In this book, the Archbishop creates awareness of how to take authority as a Christian in order to lead a blessed life as promised to them. In this book, you will find:

- Turning a curse into a blessing
- A deceivers brother
- Food and blessing
- A manipulative mother
- Stolen blessing

This book explains how people suffer unknowingly as they pay the price of sins committed by their ancestors. These sins have brought strongholds of singleness; barrenness; bad luck; incurable diseases that terminate people's lives.

Gilbert Deya explains clearly the origins of these problems, of 'generational curses' and the solutions of these 'curses' through the Blood of Jesus.

All books available from all major booksellers worldwide, and at Waterstones, WH Smiths and online at www.amazon.com and www.deyaministries.com

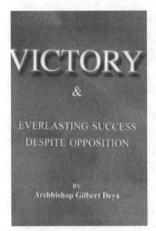

VICTORY &EVERLASTING SUCCESS DESPITE OPPOSITION

This book narrates how God made a covenant of blessing with Abraham, a righteous man, and how He is still keeping his promise of blessing to Abraham's descendants today.

It tells of the distress of Abraham's barren wife Sarah, who conceived at the old age of ninety, and tells how the Lord gave Abraham's grandson Joseph victory over his enemies, despite the opposition he went through, when you are succeeding even your blood brothers can plan to kill you.

You will learn how God's blessings flow in the lives of believers who practice holiness and righteousness and encourages believers, whose prayers remain unanswered, to be hopeful and continue to have faith in God while waiting for their miracles.

All books available from all major booksellers worldwide, and at Waterstones, WH Smiths and online at www.amazon.com and www.deyaministries.com

EFFECTIVE PRAYERS WHICH BRING SOLUTION TO PROBLEMS

Effective Prayers is a book of prayers for believers to say daily to take authority over Satan and overcome their enemies who are fighting against them.

Believers need to know how to pray effectively by pleading the blood of Jesus into specific problems which bring confusion into their lives. They need to know how to take victory through the blood of Jesus to solve problems such as wickedness, confusion, sin, the spirit of insult and suffering because of lack of knowledge. People who were suffering under witch-craft attack, people who were persecuted because of jealousy and even those who were infected with unknown sicknesses, including incurable diseases, have used this prayer book and testified that they received their breakthrough in Jesus' name.

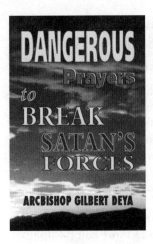

DANGEROUS PRAYERS TO BREAK SATAN'S FORCES

Psalms 35.1-4 A prayer for help

Oppose those who oppose me, LORD, and fight those who fight against me! Take your shield and amour and come to my rescue. Lift up your spear and axe against who pursue me. Promise that you will save me.

May those who try to kill me be defeated and be disgraced! May those who plot against me be turned back and be confused! [GNBI

All books available from all major book-sellers worldwide, and at Waterstones, WH Smiths and online at www.amazon.com and www.deyaministries.com

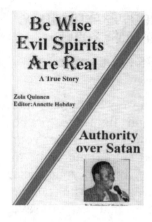

Be Wise
Evil Spirits
Are Real
A True Story

Zola Quinnen
Editor: Annette Hohday

Authority
over Satan

BE WISE EVIL SPIRITS ARE REAL

A true story

The tone of this book is very painful, but it is a reality. It triggers my feelings emotionally and I cannot hold back my tears, I then begin to ask many questions. Why did this happen to my family? Who killed my parents and why? Why did they die like that? Why did Jill not tell me earlier what she knew about my mother? Some of the most painful things I have to face are that my mum who caused most, if not all of my suffering and the man I loved, my father, are dead now. The police reported that they were stoned to death on the 19th June 1997 in front of their home. Their dogs ate their bodies, licked their blood until the relatives, police and TV crew arrived. The people who were suspected of killing my parents were arrested, but the stones used to crush their heads were so big that it was questionable and it was dismissed that they were the culprits. We buried my parents in the most expensive caskets on the 6th July 1997.

I used the word 'cruelty' to indicate the pain and suffering my mum put me through by collaborating with the Devil. Some children and adults are going through similar experience in this world. In most cases, the cause of conflicts is blamed on the individual. In this book, I agree that people have a responsibility in their lives, but I disagree that they have total control. I had no control in what was happening to me. I was only three years old when my mum gave me away to the Commander of the Demons as his wife, instructed him never to leave me until I was dead and added to this, instructed over three thousand demons to live in my stomach.

How to Receive Prosperity Miraculously

by
Archbishop
Gilbert Deya

HOW TO RECEIVE PROSPERITY MIRACULOUSLY

In this book, Archbishop Gilbert Deya combines biblical principles, with personal experiences for a powerful teaching on how to receive prosperity miraculously. There are also personal testimonies of members of his Ministry who are blessed because of his teachings. We can be successful Christians in this world. Psalms 34:10; ' Even lions go hungry for lack of food, but those who obey the LORD lack nothing good!

In Acts 19:13-20, Demons confess that they know Jesus: Some Jews who travelled round and drove out evil spirits also tried to use the name of the LORD Jesus to do this. They said to the evil spirits, "I command you in the name of Jesus, whom Paul preaches. "Seven brothers, who were the Sons of a Jewish High Priest named Sceva, were doing this. But the evil spirit said to them, "I know Jesus, and l know Paul, but you - who are you?" [GNBJ

The man who had the evil spirit in him attacked them with such violence that he overpowered them all. They ran away from his house, wounded and with their clothes torn off. All the Jews and Gentiles who lived in Ephesus heard about this; they were all filled with fear, and the name of the LORD Jesus was given greater honour. Many of the believers came, publicly admitting and revealing what they had done. Many of those who had practised magic brought their books together and burnt them in public.

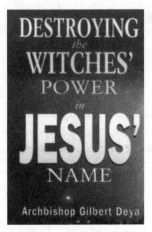

DESTROYING THE witches' POWER IN JESUS' NAME

This book explains how people suffer unknowingly as they pay the price of sins committed by their ancestors. These sins have brought strongholds of: singleness; bareness; bad luck; incurable diseases that terminate people's lives.

Gilbert Deya explains clearly the origins of these problems, of 'generational curses' and the solution of these 'curses' through the Blood of Jesus.

All books available from all major book-sellers worldwide, and at Waterstones, WH Smiths and online at www.amazon.com and www.deyaministries.com

CASTING OUT DEVILS IN JESUS' NAME

by
Archbishop
Gilbert Deya

CASTING OUT THE DEVIL IN JESUS' NAME

Evil spirits can stay inside people. They are called unclean spirits or demons or spirits of the devil. Jesus knew very well that unclean spirits were in people's lives. His ministry was a ministry that did not compromise with the devil. He came to destroy the works of Satan. That means, to cast devils out of people. Jesus gave his disciples power to cast out demons, that means move them out in the name of Jesus

All books available from all major booksellers worldwide, and at Waterstones, WH Smiths and online at www.amazon.com and www.deyaministries.com

4th July 2002
The day
Archbishop Gilbert Deya
meet the British Royal Family

Her Majesty the Queen greets Archbishop Gilbert Deya as Prince Philip, Gakuru Macharia and Amos Deya look on

Archbishop Deya
with Prince Philip, the husband of Her Majesty the Queen

Archbishop Deya
meeting with the former Kenyan President
Daniel Arap Moi

Hold fast to Jesus he
will fast.   song

Life boat resue

Better right with God

prov 18. V10 The name of
the Lord is a strong Tower etc
V 21 Death and life is in the
power of the tongue etc.
V22 who so fineth a wife fineth
a good thing and obtain favour of the
Lord. V24 a friend
prov 15 4. a wholesome tongue is
a tree of life.

January Prayer Request

1 1 Jh 3, -9. whoever is
2 born of God do not commit sin
3 v 11 v9   etc
4 James 4-8 double minded
5 v 10 humble - v 11 speak no evil
6 v 17 to good and doeth and

Thank God for answering my prayers
Answered prayers

do it not is sin.

1
2 Ps. 34 - 13 keep thy tongue
3 from evil
4 v 14 Depart from evil
5 15 The eyes of the Lord are
6 upon the righteous - 17
The R cry and the Lord heareth
them and delivereth them out
of all their ~~the~~ troubles.

February Prayer Request

1 matt 27 - V46 - 47.49
2 V52 - 54 - 55
3 Gen. 12 - 1 - V 13 Says
4 pray thee thou art my
5 sits sister etc
6 Ahram

Thank God for answering my prayers
Answered prayers

1 1Jh 4.4 Greater is he that
2 is in you than he that is in
3 the world etc
4 Jhn 16.33 I have
5 overcome the world et
6 1 tim 2 - V15 childbearing
2 Cor 4 - 18. v 7
cor 5.

March Prayer Request

1 matt 11-28 Come unto me all he
2 that labour and are heavy laden
                                          etc

3 matt 6-34
4. ECC-1 Vanity y Vanities etc
5 Luke 22 - V54 - V63 they
6 mocked him and smote him etc

Thank God for answering my prayers
Answered prayers

1 1' 2H
2 1 Pet 1 - V23
3 Matt 4, 3 The tempter came
4 in he said If thou be the son
5 g man command these stones
6 to be made bread. etc

colossian. 1-27 Christ in you the hope
of glory.

ps. 43 — Deliver me from the

deceitful and unjust man.

April Prayer Request

let not your heart be troubled

1 Matt 14 — 15 keep my command me

2 act 4 — 12

3 matt 18.

4 luke 15 — 17.

5 ○ ᵧₙ Gen 3 — 9

6

Thank God for answering my prayers
Answered prayers

1 Matt 14 & ᵐᵃᵗᵗ 15

2 matt 16.

Love 3 1 Jhn 4. — V7 Beloved let

4 us love one another etc

5 matt 25 ten virgins

6 Matt 15 VII What comes out

of the mouth this defileth a man

V14 blind cant lead blind

√ 19. etc

May Prayer Request

ʼt 1 Matt 8. v-21 Let the dead

2 bury there dead

3 Mark 5. 25 the woman

4 with the issue of blood.

5 Exodus 20 V12 Honour thy

6 father & mother that thy days

Thank God for answering my prayers
Answered prayers

may be long etc.

1 V 13, Thou shalt not kill

2 thou sall not commit adultry

3 thou shalt not steal.

4 thou shalt not bear false

5 witness against thy neighbour etc

6 Luke 11 - read. etc. ask and it

shall be given etc.

June Prayer Request

1 Hew 11 - 9 - 10 - 11

2 ~~Sarah. child.~~

3 matt 12 - 36 - 37

4 mark 11 - v13 fig tree

5 Jhn 4. 4. Greater is he

6 than in you than he that is

Thank God for answering my prayers
Answered prayers

in the world.

1 Jh16 - 23 - 24   ask the

2 father in my name he

3 shall give it.

4 Prov 19 - 15 - 25 a poor man

5 is better than a liar.

6 ps32. he who trust in the

lord mercy shall surround him

v 8 I will instruct thee and teach

thee in the way which thou shalt

July Prayer Request

1 prov 4-20 my son attend
2 to my words incline thine
3 ear into my sayings
4 Jhn 14-1-11 Let not your
5 heart be troubled. etc.
6 v15 If he love me —

Thank God for answering my prayers
Answered prayers

1 keep my commandments.
2 prov-18 Death & life is
3 in the power of the tongue
4 ps 81 - 10 Open thy
5 mouth wide and I will
6 fill it.

mark 11-23-24.

I will guide thee. I will guide thee

August Prayer Request

1 Jh. 3 V 8. he that
2 committed sin is of the
3 devil. etc.
4 Acts 10 - 38 How God
5 anionted Jesus of
6 nazareth. etc

Thank God for answering my prayers
Answered prayers

Luke 10 mery & martha V 41

1 Malachi 3 V 8
2 Joshua 1 Take possession
3 of your blening
4 numbers
5 1 Pet 5-3 God resisteth
6 the ~~peer~~ proud and giveth
grace to the humble
1 Cor 7 about marrage

September Prayer Request

1. Rev 22 . 17
2. Colossian 3—1
3. Luke 6—35 v 37 —46 Lord Lord.
4. Isiah 55 —10 —11
5. It shall not return to me
6. void.

Thank God for answering my prayers
Answered prayers

1. Luke 12 —V 13
2. James 1 —V 8 a double
3. minded man is un stable
4. in all is ways.
5. JH8—31—59
6. Prov 20 . V 27 The ~~candle~~ spirit of
man is the candle of the
Lord searching all the in ward
parts of the belly

October Prayer Request

1 Ps 50 everthing is is etc

2 ps 59

3 James 1-22 bat be ye

4 doeb.

5 Jhn 4-29 come see

6 man etc.

Thank God for answering my prayers
Answered prayers

1 Due 28

2 Luke 9. V35 this is my

3 beloved son, hear him.

4 1 Peter 2-24 grass

5 1 John 5-11-12.

6 Luke 22. V61-71.

Isiah 55-11 it shall not
return unto
Isiah 54-17 me void
no weapon.

November Prayer Request

1 Heu 11-V10, For he looked

2 for a city which hath

3 foundations whose builder

4 & maker is God.

5 Is 41

6

Thank God for answering my prayers
Answered prayers

Heu 4 V12 For the word

1 of God etc.

2 2 tim 3-16-17

3 2 Cor 9-V6

4 Ep. 6-11

5 1 Pet 2-9 But we are

6 a choosen generation etc

Eph. 5-V14

December Prayer Request

1 Psa 10. v21 The lips of the
2 prov righteous feed many etc
3 v22 The blessing of the Lord
4 it maketh rich and he added
  no sorrow with it.
5 v30 The righteous. shall never
6 be removed etc

Thank God for answering my prayers
Answered prayers

prov 8 -33 hear instruction
1 Hosea -4-6 Suffer
2 my people are desty
3 for lack of knowledge
4 coloss 2
5 " 3 risen with
6 christ
2 Co 18 all things are of God

matt 28 19-20)

Mark 5-V 41. What manner g
man is this that even the wind
and sea obey him

Rev 12 V 15 And the serpent
cant g his mouth water etc
Jh 14 - V 14 If he shell ask any
thing in my name I will do ct.

Ep 4 - 19. But my God
shall supply all   etc

Jh 19 - 21 write not the k
g Jews but that he said
    etc

— eccles 12 - V 13 Fear God and
keep #15 commandment for the
whole duty g man is to serve
God. etc. 8

pro 4 read

Is 48 V22 There is no peace
saith the Lord unto the wicked
etc.

V 17 Thus saith the Lord thy
redeemer the holy one of Israel
etc

Heb 11-24 By faith etc.
25 choosing rather to suffer
affliction with the people etc

ps 116 V 11 I said in my haste all
men are liars.

p118. V5. I called upon the Lord etc
v6 the Lord is on my side I will
not fear what can man do unto
me, etc V17 I shall not die
but live to declare the works of
the Lord. etc V19 Open to me
the gates of righteousness. I
will go into them and I will praise
the Lord. V22. The stone.

V 24 This the day that the
V25 etc

V 28 thou art my God and I will
praise ~~him~~ thee
V 29 O give thanks etc.

- ps 125. They that trust in the Lord
shall be as mount Zion which
cannot be removed but abideth
for ever. etc.

EXO 23. V 24

2 Cor 5 ~~-17~~ therefore if any
man be in christ he is a new
creature etc.

Rom 8. V 28 and we know
that all things work together for
good to them that love God to etc
V 31 If God be for us who
can be against us. etc.
V 37 Nay in all these things we conquerors
etc

Rom - 13.

<u>Gal 6.</u> ~3 For if a man think himself to be something when he is nothing he deceiveth himself. etc.

V7 Be not deceived God is not mocked for whatsoever a man soweth that shall he also reap etc

V5 For every man shall bear his own burden

V6. Let him that is taught in the word communicate unto him that teacheth in all good things

V9 . And let us not be weary in well doing.

<u>Psalm 34.</u> V #6 The ~~face~~ of the Lord is against them that do evil etc.

v17 the righteous cry and the Lord hear~~eth them~~ and delivereth them out of all their troubles. etc.

<u>Ps.113.</u> V3 From the rising of the sun to the going down of the same etc

<u>Phil 4.19.</u> Supply our needs